# FINDING TEDDY

by

*Theodore G. Pough*

Publish by Cinematic Soul Press

ISBN 979-8-218-83339-8

Cover and interior design by Theodore G. Pough
Printed in the United  States of America
First Edition

For those who speak from silence,
and find rhythm in the quiet.
For every poet, dreamer, and midnight soul
who turns solitude into song,
and for the inner child who still whispers beneath the noise,
reminding us that softness survives.
This is for us.

# Table of Contents

## *We're Going*

# WHERE WE ARE...

## The Body Learns

As far back as memory breathes,
it was the body of a man that caught my eye.
Not with hunger.
Not with thirst.
But with amazement—
a reverence for muscle stretched over bone,
for arms veined like rivers,
for strength carved into something almost grown.

Wrestling superstars parading on the screen,
chests aglow, fists mean,
and to me (a boy not yet called by name),
questions bloomed like heat through every frame,
watching, wondering, worshipping the flame.

And the girls, they were there too:
sweet, melodic, fresh as dew,
wrapped in scents of springtime's bloom,
but too sacred, too far across the room.
Maybe it was my mama's voice,
sharp as slammed doors, offering no choice
that taught me early:
some things are too tender for boys like me to carry.

So I learned not to reach.
Not to crave.
Just ignore
the sacred wave.

But later, it was easier to lean into men,
the ones who didn't shiver when my story was told.
Easier to let the gravity of that man's body
pull me under without shame.

It wasn't forced.
I wasn't broken.
I was choosing.

Choosing doors that wouldn't splinter at my touch.
Choosing hands that wouldn't tremble too much.
Choosing survival over dreams that cost too much.

And girls, they did like me.
Said I was sweet.
Brushed my arm in long lines down the hall.

But I was slow, slow to feel,
heartbeats lagging behind the wheel.
By the time I looked up,
she had moved on
but Lord knows I wanted her, wanted her all along.
Wanted the softness in her gaze,
the way her voice melted into praise.

And I knew natural rhythm of things that were taught—
man and woman, seed and thought.
I knew it all,
but my hands couldn't move to it.

But secretly,
I wanted men too
not for their hard dicks and plump asses,
or for what pleasure they could offer,
but rather for their blessed hands
the ones to hold you firm against your own unrest.
A father's grip, a brother's shove,
a touch that said:
you are enough, manhood validated!
But sex was the only door that stayed unlocked,
the only way I thought I could talk.

So I may have been lusting for her touch,
a chance to taste her sweet juices
that only her pussy could bring.
But, I settled for his instead,
But not really.
What I craved for was more:
not bodies, but belonging,

---

not skin, but a longing,
not lust, but a place to land.
Not conquest....but hugs.

The first touches came in the way storms do:
fast, half-sweet, half-rude.
A crackling voice on a line that bled static,
a body under a bridge, fevered and frantic.
A man in a car.
A man too large.
A man who filled this hollow before I knew how to charge.

They taught me how to stretch,
how to hold breath,
how to become a temple with no one inside.
I learned how to nod without needing a heart.
I learned how to say "yes" while standing apart.

The body learns before the heart does.

How to open,
how to bend,
how to carry
what it cannot yet understand.

## Rare Candy

I wasn't built for battles—
not at first.
I was the quiet one in the tall grass,
rooted deep,
hoping not to be seen,
hoping someone would see me.

They said:
*Pick fire. Pick flash. Pick strength.*
I chose Bulbasaur—
patient, grounded,
growing in silence,
fighting with sunlight
and stillness.

I didn't evolve on command.
Didn't rush the glow-up.
I held my power like a seed,
watered it slowly.
Let it bloom when I was ready.

I didn't burn bright—
I lingered.
Hung back like fog in the morning.
Not everyone saw me.
But those who did?
Felt me.

They gave me TMs
that didn't fit my type.
Tried to reprogram my softness
into something more marketable.
But you can't code the quiet magic
of a Ghost-type soul—
how it phases in and out,
how it disappears just enough
to stay whole.

And here's the truth they never tell you:
even Pikachu said no to the stone.
And Eevee had choices.

I fainted in love.
Ran from fights.
Got hexed by expectations.
Paralyzed by doubt,
burned by silence,
frozen out of friend circles.

However, I always healed.
Made it back to the center.
Kept walking through the tall grass,
heart like a Pokéball—
cracked, but still catching wonder.

Until I found the ones
who didn't need me to evolve,
just wanted me to stay.

And now?

Now I don't chase badges.
I don't beg to be caught.
I roam free.
Wild and worthy.
One of one.

Call me legendary.
Not because I had to evolve,
but because I stayed true
to the form I was born to love.

## Kindness Shouldn't Feel Like Harm

Maya Angelou once said:
*If someone shows you who they are, believe them.*

I say, "bullshit."

Because why is it,
every time you quote that line,
you already knew what time it was
but ignored the red flags anyway?

At the same time—
someone kind shows up.
Genuine.
Soft-spoken.

And what do we do?

We flinch.
We squint.
We scan for the scam—
like kindness is a hustle
from the last chapter.

We don't trust sweet no more.
Can't sit with care.
Too used to silence,
or sex,
or someone who's only there
until the thrill cools
and the mask slips off.

We don't believe in "good,"
we wait for the loss.

And maybe Maya was right.
Maybe truth shows up early—
but trauma hits first
and makes our vision blurry.

Maybe we were taught
to read people like threats—
red flags waving
in skin and breath.

So when someone brings warmth,
we check the exits.
And when they say "I got you,"
we second-guess it.

I've pushed good people away too.
Didn't know what to do
with open arms.

Didn't trust what didn't come
with chaos,
with charm,
with a chase.

I called steady boring.
Thought peace was a trap
in a clean smile.

So I left first.
Or I tested them.
Or I made them prove
what I should've just received.

I've mistaken red flags
for red lights I ran through,
hoping I'd beat the crash.
I've misread softness as bait—
and distance as class.

I've been wrong.
Not just about them—
but about me.
about what I thought
love was supposed to be.

I've cussed out good love
for showing up late.
Blocked blessings
because they didn't flirt right.
Let my guard down for the devil
'cause he knew my favorite lies.
And still—
I want more.
Still—
I ache for soft.

So yeah—
maybe kindness don't come loud.
Maybe it don't come sexy.
Maybe it don't come when you want it.

But when it comes?
Let it!

Let it hold you
like nothing's wrong.
Let it kiss your scars
like they still sing.
Let it stay.

Because kindness
ain't harm.
It's the healing
you didn't know how to ask for.

## The Kind That Lingers

Whatever happened to courtship?
To that slow unfolding—
the space between sweaty palms
and sacred vows,
where love learns your laugh
before it memorizes your body.

Where the date don't end at midnight
just because the food's gone.
Where we linger in doorways,
talk 'til the streetlights start yawning,
and I forget to check my phone
because you're saying something
worth staying for.

I want to smell the rose you gave me
and remember that hidden garden
you swore would change my mind—
and it did.
Because anything touched by your intention
blooms.

I want to fight sleep on work calls
'cause last night I stayed up
to hear your voice fold over mine.
Not even talking—
just knowing you were there
on the other side of the line,
breathing steady.
That's the kind of prayer I dream in.

And just like Aretha—
I want to make you
feel like a natural woman.
Be your Doctor Feelgood
in the morning,
never leave you wondering
if there ain't no way to love me,
because the truth is—

I do need you.
I need slow.
I need deliberate.
I need effort without being begged for.

I want the kind of love
that's fluent in Tuesday.
That folds laundry without asking.
That texts "You good?"
and means it.
That holds my face when I can't hold it together.
That brings me tea with the right amount of honey
just because.

I want that lake scene from Jason's Lyric—
the hush of water holding us while the world forgets our names.
No script.
Just mouths learning each other's language
with the patience of poets.

Your hands exploring—not claiming—
skin I forgot could respond.

My hips arch,
not for performance,
but from how you look at me
like a *yes* you've been waiting to earn.

We undress,
not just clothes,
but memory.

And when you trace my spine
like it's scripture,
I stop bracing for the burn.

This isn't lust.
This is legacy.

You, steady as moonlight.

Me, shivering with belief.

Two Black bodies,
barefoot on sacred ground,
naming each other in the dark
and calling it safe.

Love doesn't have to be loud.
But it should echo.
Should hum through the day's small silences
and leave fingerprints
in forgotten places.

Whatever happened to courtship?
To learning my favorite side of the bed
before climbing into it?
To showing up with more
than just promises and playlists?

I'm not asking for grand.
I'm asking for real.
For rhythm.
For attention that doesn't flinch.

Because when love lingers,
so do I.

## Before the Heart Does

And somewhere along the way,
I forgot how to pray
forgot the scent of lilac wrists,
forgot the dream of that girl's shy kiss,
forgot the laughter trembling on buttons undone,
forgot the softness made for someone.

Men became an easy gospel,
loud, rough, apostle by apostle.
I built a body count enough to fill pews,
but no woman ever sang in that raucous, rough muse.

And so here I am
still a virgin to the sacred plan.
Still untouched by the thing I thought was mine.
Still wondering if the door closed in time,
while I was busy trading ache for touch,
and dreams for rush.

Maybe the door to her touch is closed.
Maybe it isn't; maybe it only froze.
Maybe some doors never lock,
just waiting patient with ticking clocks.

Maybe I was never too broken.
Never too split, never misspoken.

Maybe tenderness doesn't care for the counts,
or the bodies, or the bounced amounts.
Maybe it only listens to the pulse,
to the longing,
to the trembling waltz.

I am still here.
Still humming.
Still pulsing.
Still longing.

Still believing there's a softness somewhere that knows my name —
and if she ever comes,
if she presses her palm to my chest and whispers,
*You were always worthy.*

Maybe
just maybe
the heart will finally learn
what the body's carried all this time.

## GREEN LINE

Gentrification couldn't whitewash this feeling of love.

Remember when you kissed me at the U Street stop, right before the train came—like the city was ours?

Every stop felt like a pause in time, just me and you, nothing else but the smell of incense and Go-Go in the air.

Even the Metro lights felt like candlelight when your hand found mine and held on past Gallery Place.

Nothing holy about the ride, but damn if it didn't feel like prayer.

Leaning in, you touched me—and joy rippled through me like a street performer's secret smile when the crowd moves with him.

It was more than a flirt—it was choreography written by hands that had learned me in silence.

Next thing I knew, I was believing again—

Even if just for a few stops, I called it love.

## Yo Man Yo Man

It was never my intention
to put you in this position
between the man you love
and your best friend.

I didn't ask for this division,
this blurred-line living.
I just wanted your heart,
not a courtroom decision.

But here we are.
A line clearly drawn,
yet somehow,
it fades when the vibe gets strong.

'Cause if your friend is your friend
and I'm yo man, yo man, yo man...
then why do I still feel like I'm in the stands
watching y'all pass notes in a game
I thought I started?

Where does the problem lie
unless therein lies a problem
too complex for Aunt Sally to solve
even with all her parentheses and PEMDAS pride?

I ain't hatin'.
Really, I'm not.
It's a beautiful thing,
the bond y'all got.
Loyalty like that?
Rare in a world that tosses people
like half-read texts at 2am.

But I can't lie
sometimes it stings
how easily y'all sync,
how he gets the raw you

while I get the rehearsed script.
I know I'm worth the full showing,
not just the edited cut.
Not just the good-night texts
and the polite I miss you's
but the sweat,
the stammer,
the unfiltered pulse
of wanting someone so bad
you forget who called first.

I came second in a race
I didn't know I was running.
Is your heart first-come, first-serve?
Or do I gotta RSVP
and pray there's space left at the table?

I'm not tryna break that bond
just asking:
"Where do I belong?"

Am I the lover
or the guest star
who shows up every third episode
while the series stays loyal to its original cast?

And maybe I'm insecure.
Maybe I need to chill.
But if I'm the one you undress for,
why does he get the realest version of you, still?
Why does he get the sighs between your words,
the way your voice dips when you're tired and true?
I get the soft skin,
but he gets the soul.
And I want both.

So I do what I always do
I step back,
leave the door cracked,
hope you notice the air shift.

You never do.
And little by little,
I become the shadow
you used to kiss.

Sad, yeah.
But not bitter.
Not broken.
Just tired of squinting
through blurry lines
trying to make out my place in your picture.

So I let the silence speak.
Let your name stay in my throat
but not on my tongue.

I fade—not ghost,
just... dim.
Just gone.
And when you wonder
why the room feels colder
just know
I was the warmth
you never reached for.

## Comfort Zone

You open the door like a ritual.
Like your body remembers
what your pride won't say.

I step in like I earned this.
I didn't.
I just know when to show up
Midnight, mostly.
Hungry.
Hollowed out by other people's needs.

I fuck you
like I'm clocking out of survival
trying to forget how many masks I wear
before I reach your lips.

And you let me.
Every time.
No lock. No questions.
Just sweat and surrender.

That's your love language, right?
Mine is exit.
You got candles.
I got excuses.

Deadlines.
Mama's sick.
Phone on *Do Not Disturb*
but I just be scrolling.

You say I don't feel nothing.
That's a lie!
I feel your throat tighten
when I don't kiss you after.
I feel your spine curve back—
not just from pleasure but from holding me
like I'm something that might stay.

I feel you watching me
like I might become worthy.

I learned touch
before I learned tenderness.
Learned how to unzip, not how to stay.
I was raised by men who left footprints,
never fingerprints.

So when you ask me
what *this* is
I pretend you're joking.
Change the subject.
Grab your ass.
Buy time with skin.

But I see you now—quiet.
Your laughter used to bounce
off the walls like it belonged here.
Now it visits like it's checking the time.
Wondering when it should leave.

Still, I text.
Still show up.
Still break you open
like a ritual
I ain't brave enough to name.

And in the stillness
after climax—
when our chests sync
and I almost tell you my real name—

I panic.
Put on my shirt.
Say, "You good?"
Even though you're not.
You never were.
Not for this.

But I'll be back.

———————————————

## Sex Siren: Ten

I was only a Ten—
but baby, that was enough
to make gods blush
and mortals rush
to taste the flame
they swore they'd never touch.

I am your Sex Siren.
The thirst you don't name.
I go deep—
past the breath, past the game.
Beyond what's safe,
where pleasure turns to shame.

Your release?
Mine to give.
Even when I'm the one
left forgetting how to live.

Judges—what's your score?
Ten for the look,
and another for the soul I took
without a single finger lifted,
just a glance that left you shifted.

So what does that make me?

A perfect Ten!
Again and again.

No one looks like me.
Hooks like me.
Reads you like a song,
then leaves you longing all night long.

But none of you
kiss me after the lights come up.
You unzip, then dip—

I stay stuck.

You vanish into daylight like nothing was spoken.
I sit in the dark, still halfway open.

And when the sun rises,
I leave you smitten
bare, blinking,
bitten by a night
you'll never admit being in.

That one over there?
He's a dime, for sure!
But me?

You got a Ten right here!
And the next category is...

Companion Realness.

You cling to me
like your life depends on it,
whispering "Hercules, Hercules"
when your grip turns frantic,
your truth slips: semantic.

And when it's done,
we drift into that hush
where names don't follow
and time turns to dust.

Minutes melt like years.
Still—
they always leave,
don't they?

Judges... what's your score?

## Small Energy

You want love.
I want pressure
ass cheeks pressed to drywall,
sweat turning paint to memory.
You call it a vibe.
I call it survival
with good lighting.

You want plans.
I want dick.
You want to be kissed slow.
I want to be swallowed
whole,
then forgotten
before sunrise.

Your breath smells like Listerine and want.
Mine?
Hennessy and boundary issues.
You hum while folding my shirt.
I fake sleep
so I don't have to hold your hope.

I know your spine by fingertip.
But your last name?
Slips my mind
like your boxers
did last time.
I've mapped your back with my mouth
but never learned the curve of your pain.

You write poems about me.
I screenshot them,
smile,
and fuck someone else
in the same socks you complimented.

You say I feel like church.

I say,
"say it again
with your hand on my chest"
so I can pretend
this is worship
and not withdrawal.

You ask for softness.
I bring lube.
You want music.
I bring moans
that don't know your name.

I like your patience,
but I crave noise.
I like your calm,
but only in the rearview.
You want rhythm.
I bring sweat
with no chorus.

You say you're tired
of being a secret.
But baby,
you knew the shape of this silence
before you pressed your ear to it.

You want warmth.
I want what's warm.
You want presence.
I want the storm.

Don't confuse this chaos
for chemistry.
It's not a promise.
It's performance.

But goddamn—
you taste like truth
even when I lie.

# Never The One

You hit me up,
late, of course.
The kind of late that hums lust
and nothing else.

No *how you been?*
No *good mornings.*
Just
*What you doing?*
like my time folds for you.

And I used to love it;
the thrill, the excitement of
how your voice
sounds like velvet
pulled tight across my spine.
How your hands
answered questions
I never dared to ask out loud.

You made me feel seen
in the dark.
But daylight tells another story.

I don't want you.
Not really.
I want to be wanted—
in public,
in plans,
in places where I'm not a secret.

You call it vibes.
I call it being convenient
to someone who never arrives fully.

You say *I know the deal.*
I do.
But that doesn't make it holy.

I used to whisper your name
like a spell—
hoping the moan
might turn sacred.
But it never does.
It's always
his breath hot on my neck,
fingertips carving *yes* into skin,
then silence so loud
my bones forget they were touched.

Still warm from where you laid,
I gather my underwear from the floor
like picking up evidence
of a crime no one will report.

I got dressed in front of mirrors
you never looked into.
Brushed off my worth
like lint from sheets you left behind.

But some of us crave more
than bare skin
and an open door
after 11 p.m.

I don't want flowers.
I want presence.
Not forever.
Just honesty.

Not love.
Just respect.

So tonight?
Keep your *U up?*
Keep your detours
and dimly lit affection.

I've retired from being a good time

with bad timing.

I'm not your secret.
Not anymore.
I was never asking to be everything—
just not the thing you reach for
when the world is asleep
and you remember
I exist.

## The Work

We lay there—breathless, spent.
He fucked me good, and he knew it.
Had me gushing in places I didn't know I had,
climbing walls that would remember our names.

He felt it too—
which is why he was quiet.
Only difference:
my eyes saw a future,
his saw routine.

A clock in,
then a clock out.
We were doing the work.
But there was no bonus
for love.

Haiku:

He had me gushing—
I begged to be called beloved.
His words were silent.

## Rush Hour at 2 AM

I used to call it magic...
the way the room would bend
when the rush hit.
Heartbeat doing double-dutch
with the sweat on my back.
Head loose. Breath shallow.
Everything golden for a second.

That's when I'd let him in.
Sometimes a stranger.
Sometimes a name I kept
under "almost,"
But always a yearning in disguise.

Still lightheaded from the hit,
I wipe myself clean with my shirt
underwear twisted like shame on the floor,
a scene I've replayed
in browser tabs and backrooms,
chasing climax  like it holds a cure.

Porn became my morning ritual—
not desire,
but the illusion of being chosen.
I learned their moans by name,
inserted my being in scenes
where everyone got touched
without shame.

I wasn't getting off.
I was getting even
with the silence.

And the poppers—
Lord, the poppers—
sweet poison perfume
that made the whole room
go soft around the edges.

I'd hit...then drift.
Float past the fact
that I felt nothing
even when I was being touched.

You ever fuck just to remember
what your body's for?
Let someone call you beautiful
with their mouth full of need
and still feel like a hallway
with no doors?

I became a ritual—
lit candles for men
who never looked me in the eyes.
Offered ass like communion.
Took praise as payment.

Afterwards, I'd lay there,
orgasm still wet on my belly,
wondering if anyone could see
the void pulsing beneath my skin.

And still,
I text them back.
Open the app.
Light the candle.
Wait.

The room smells like sweat
 and someone else's cologne.
I lay back, legs parted like punctuation—
waiting for the sentence to finish itself.

3:05 AM.
And I am still here.
Still watching.
Still wanting.
Still...not enough.

## 3:05 AM

I roll over,
reach for a body
I've never actually touched—
but swear I've held in dreams.

So when the bed turns cold,
I turn to the warmth of the phone—
light the candle
like I'm summoning something
other than silence.
Rush in one hand.
A deep inhale.
I swear the ghosts go quiet for a second.

2:18 AM.
He arrives.
No name.
No questions.
Just the scent of a man
trying not to remember who he is.
Same as me.

We undress like we're erasing something.
Not lust.
Just grief in motion.

2:30 AM.
He fucks like he means it.
Like the louder I moan,
the less I'll ask after.
His hips knock truth out of me—
I arch, pretend it's ecstasy.
But I'm just stretching the silence,
hoping friction can do what words won't.

He's in me.
Or I'm in him.
Doesn't matter.

We're somewhere between skin and survival.

I moan on command.
Theatrical.
Lush.
I say his name like I mean it—
but I'm thinking of someone
who used to trace my chest like scripture
and call it prayer.

3:05 AM.
He finishes.
Fast.
Hands on my ass
like I'm something he stole
and doesn't plan to keep.

I don't cum for the man.
I cum for the pause—
the breath between ache and apology.
And afterward,
when he wipes his hands
like I was something he spilled,
I smile.
Because at least I made a mess.

3:37 AM.
He leaves.
Door doesn't close all the way.
Like he might return.
He won't.

I lay there,
legs still open,
mouth tasting nothing.
The screen on my phone lights up—
porn paused at the part
where someone kisses
like they mean it.
The silence returns

like a jealous ex—
arms folded,
watching me pretend this is enough.
It always shows up
after the last kiss lands
like a receipt I can't return.

4:00 AM.
I say I'm done.
Again.
Blow out the candle.
Lie back down.

I reach for my phone
before the bed goes cold.

## I Still Believe

I've been touched
but not held.
Admired, but not protected.
Known by the flesh,
but never remembered by the heart.

And I keep asking:
why do we do this to each other?
Same wounds, same scars—
and still, we cut.

Is it because we were never given gentleness,
so we never learned how to give it?
Is it survival?
Is it shame in drag?
Is it fear that if we don't strike first,
we'll be the one left bleeding?

I've been kissed like a mirror.
Loved like a secret.
Fucked like a favor someone thought I owed.
I've opened my door to brothers
who only came to take something soft
and leave before it could speak.

I've been told my kindness is too much.
My softness, suspicious.
My silence...something to fill,
not something to understood.

And still, I ask:
Why are we like this?
Why do we ghost each other like ancestors'
names we were never taught to say?
Why do we burn bridges we never had
and call it a boundary?

---

Maybe I'm not supposed to know.
Maybe none of us do.
Maybe the trauma runs so deep,
it dreams for us even while sleep.

Maybe we all walked through fire
and forgot how to stop flinching.
Maybe love sounds like a threat
when you've only ever known silence or sex.

I don't have answers.
Only bruises and questions.
Only memories of nights I needed a friend
but got a stranger's body instead.

I'm not mad at us.
Just tired.
Tired of calling it strength
when we're really just scared.
Tired of calling it preference
when it's simply pain wearing cologne.

What if we made space?
Not just for bodies—
but for sorrow,
for silence,
for second chances?

What if we held one another
without always needing to have each other?
What if we slow desire down,
just long enough to hear one another's name?

What if we built something?
Not clubs.
Not cliques.
But communion—
where soft boys, loud boys, femme boys,
tired boys, churchy boys, broken boys

could all just be boys
while figuring out how to become men?

What if we grieved together?
What if we remembered Marlon, Essex, Joseph,
and every boy who died waiting to be loved
without apology?

What if healing wasn't a solo sport,
but a team huddle,
a group prayer,
a night where nobody gets left on read?

So I'll go first.
I vow to be softer,
even when the world tells me that's stupid.
I'll stay kind,
even if it gets mistaken for weakness.

I'll speak "I miss you"
before it turns to resentment.
I'll check on my brothers
before they become strangers.
I'll hold space,
even when mine is empty.

And if I fall—
if I love too hard,
or trust too quick,
or reach out and get nothing back—
I won't call it a failure.
I'll call it a seed.

Because I still believe
we can learn to treat each other right.

Even if no one taught us.
Even if we're still healing.
Even if we're scared.

I still believe.

## Red Line

What happens to a dream when realized?

Does it bloom
like a fresh rose in May?

Or haunt you
as potential left to fade away?

Is it a reminder of the impossible?
Or a call to the hungry,
enticed by the scent of something sweet?

Perhaps it waits
for someone to truly see it.

Or does bitterness
become its fate?

*...HOW WE ARE*

## Before I Had The Words

Before I had the words, I smiled for no reason.
Imagination was my secret escape.
Felt my wings lifting off to touch the sky.
Walking as royalty down a runway.
Tasted the sweetest pear that tastes like joy.
Excited for Christmas morning, waking up to presents.
Looking up at the country night sky in wonderment.
Bringing home a trophy just to brag.
Giving my mom a card for her day.
Picking dandelions to make a bouquet.

## The Rules They Gave Us

Where I come from,
little boys didn't wear pink—
we didn't even say the word.

We didn't play with dolls,
and we didn't dream out loud.
We were handed a ball
we didn't ask for,
and told, *Go outside. Be a boy.*
Even if you weren't built for that game.

I never picked it up.
Didn't fake the dribble.
Didn't chase the cheers.
But I learned the plays—
Stay quiet. Stay tough.
Stay in line.

They didn't tell us to dream—
they told us to survive.
To clock in. To muscle through.
To trade brilliance for bread.

Be book smart, but don't get too deep.
Be talented, but don't your waste time
with that art stuff.

Paintings don't pay the bills.
Poems don't fix the roof.
Songs don't put food on the table—
unless you're famous, or white.

You could be a dancer
as long as it got you close to women.
A singer,
as long as the falsetto doesn't sound too sweet.

We praised boys who could move—
but only if it looked like hustle,
not healing.

The dreamers got folded into labor.
The readers into routine.
We built strength in our backs
while our minds starved.

But I made it.
By refusing to bury the soft, strange spark
they told me to kill.
Not by grinding myself to the bone.

No,
I still don't wear pink—
but I rock yellow with pride.
Not loud, but alive.
Not for fashion, but for freedom.

I found liberation
not in lifting weight,
but in lifting words.
By writing what I was never allowed to say.
In dreaming
without asking for permission.

I don't sweat for my worth anymore.
I speak it.
I craft it.
I live it.

And every poem I write
is a shift in the foundation—
proof that the boy
who was told to *get real*
chose, instead,
to get free.

## Trapped in the Temple

The place I once called sanctuary
feels more like a cemetery—
a place where dreams died
after living a purposeful life.
Only problem is
it was just my imagination—
a thousand lives over
from this pew,
praying for a thousand more.

My thoughts echo like choirboys in mourning,
singing hymns for futures that never arrived.
Every window here is stained with what-ifs.
Every bell tower holds the ghost of who I could've been.

I am Quasimodo in my own skull,
ringing alarms no one hears—
swinging from thought to thought
like hunch-backed hope
strung up in high-ceilinged arches,
watching joy dance in the courtyard below,
but never stepping outside.

The place I once called sanctuary
is now a stage for shame in robes—
Claude Frollo pacing the pulpit of my brain,
calling every desire a sin,
every longing a fire I must drown.

He tells me Esmeralda is a distraction,
says her laughter is dangerous,
that her hips spell downfall,
her joy is witchcraft,
her freedom—a seduction
meant to undo all the walls I've built
around this holy ache.

And I believed him.

Let the guilt dress up as guidance.
Let the voice that feared beauty
named me blessed.
Let the saboteur be my shepherd.

The place I once called sanctuary
smells like old incense and new resentment.
Smells like "maybe next time"
and "be grateful it's not worse."
Smells like all the songs I never danced to
because I was too busy being devout
to doubt.

I've built serveral cathedrals
in the bones of my solitude—
frescoes of fantasies,
chandeliers made of memories
that never happened.

I hear the organ playing but...
it's just my breath catching in silence.
The congregation is gone.
Only shame stays behind
to clean the floors
and lock the doors.

This place I once called my sanctuary
keeps the sunlight out on purpose.
It lets me worship my potential
but never walk in it.
Lets me light candles
but not feel their warmth.
Lets me pray for freedom
as long as I don't take a step toward it.

And still—
I kneel.

Still, I whisper psalms
to the little boy who thought
being smart was the safest way to be seen.

Still, I light incense
for the man who thought
his silence was the sacrifice
God would reward.

This place I once called my sanctuary
didn't burn down when I left—
just flickered.
Like it knew I might return.

I left through the doors trembling,
not sure if I was walking away
or being sent out.

The sunlight didn't celebrate my exit.
It just was—
indifferent and warm,
like a lover I forgot how to touch.

Outside, the wind didn't praise my leaving.
But I could breathe deeper.
And sometimes, that's enough.

Still, the shadow stretches long.
Still, I hear Frollo when the silence gets loud.
Still, I catch myself tracing patterns
on blank walls.

And some nights,
when freedom feels too quiet
and joy too loud—

I think about going back.

But I don't.
Not yet.

## Coming Home

Every day is the same.
I wake up, brush my teeth, shower,
skip breakfast,
then catch the train into work.

Work for 8 hours.
Then take the train home.

Same seat. Same silence.
Scrolling past lives I'm not living.

I walk through the door to no one—
drop my keys, kick off my shoes,
microwave something quiet.

But sometimes, I imagine you here.

Just like my mother,
asking how school was—
how my day went.
I'd say, "I passed my test.
I think I got an A."

Only now, the test is surviving the day
without falling apart.

And you'll nod, that quiet smile,
already reheating leftovers.
We sit on the couch, knees touching—
talking trash over *Real Housewives of Atlanta*.
You roll your eyes at Kenya,
laugh when I quote NeNe,
"Now why am I in it?"
Like we say it in unison.

You'll ask, "Did you eat today?"
And I lie and say "yes,"
just to watch you fix my plate anyway.

Then we'll lie in bed
legs tangled, words low.
Make love like it's our last night on earth.
Not loud, just honest.
Our bodies writing poems across skin
until sleep folds us in.

And in the morning
we do it all again.

Brush teeth. Shower.
Skip breakfast. Take the train.
Only now...

I walk through the door alone.
No plate. No laugh. No touch.
Just the hum of the fridge
and the silence of a one-bedroom dream.

But I still set the table for two.
Still fluff the pillows on your side.
Still leave the bathroom light on
like you're on your way.

And if you are,
I'll be home
when you get here.

## Daylight Doesn't Want Me

I only come through
when the moon can't tell on me.
Daylight doesn't want me.
Not the way he did—
asking what I'm hungry for
and meaning more than food.

I dip out before morning
so I don't have to taste
what I'm missing.
Leave before the sun
can name the pain
I've been dressing up as desire.

He asked me once,
"What are we doing?"
And I smiled.
Because if I said "nothing,"
it would hurt us both.
And if I said "something,"
I might have meant it.

So I stay moving.
I ghost before I can be seen.
Before my softness shows.
Before my voice cracks
when I ask,
"Do you want me to stay?"
and pray he says "no."

Because the truth is—
I like him.
I like the way his silence feels like safety.
I like how he never rushes me
to be whole.

But like always—
I keep one foot in the shadows.
One eye on the door.
One hand on the mask.

I want to be held
and I don't know how to ask.
So I fuck instead
and then disappear
before he can love the parts
I never learned to look at.

Daylight doesn't want me.
Because I'm still learning
to want myself.

## Invitation

My eyes see you —
skin glowing like sin wrapped in moonlight,
veins glimmering beneath the surface
Like candle wax ready to melt.

You taste like dusk before the dawn,
a pulse beating through silence,
and I can feel it calling me closer,
inviting my hunger to remember its name.

This isn't lust.
It's liturgy.
I don't just want your mouth—
I want your trembling,
your shiver between surrender and salvation.
I want to feed where devotion meets delirium.

Like the old ones, I wait half-shadowed.
Fangs damp with restraint.
The hunger is centuries deep,
a gospel I've swallowed
but never digested.

You must invite me in.
That's the law.
That's the curse.
So I linger at your door,
watching your breath rise and fall
like incense in the temple of your body.

When I perform,
it's not theater—it's invocation.
Like Lestat under velvet lights,
I bare my spirit in basslines,
slip my tongue through sonnets,
and let rhythm do what prayer never could.

Each stanza is a slow bite.
Each rhyme is a pulse against your throat.

---

I want to taste your story—
the one you hide behind laughter,
the one that trembles between your thighs.

I want the way your breath stutters
when my voice crawls down your spine.
The way your body opens
like scripture on the last line of confession.
The way you whisper my name
as if afraid it might save you.

Because I've stood too long
outside warm rooms,
watching others bathe in what I've only worshipped.
Rooms filled with hands,
and lips,
and laughter that doesn't fear its own shadow.

Let me in.
Not just your space—
but your pulse, your ritual, your ruin.
Let me sip the darkness
that curls beneath your smile.
Let me taste the secret you've never said aloud.

And when I drink—
let it not be your blood,
but your truth,
your surrender,
your yes that glows red in the dark.

So open the door.
Let the candlelight spill between us.
Let me step into your shadow
and make it sing.

Let me cross that threshold—
slowly, reverently—
until night itself forgets
which of us is the sinner.

## Sanctum

Come closer.
I've seen you pacing the perimeter—
eyes hollow with hunger,
spirit cloaked in centuries of silence.
You wear solitude like it's stitched to your skin,
but I know the scent
of someone searching for more.

You, too, have tasted
the shallow drip of midnight liaisons,
have fed on flesh
that couldn't nourish your name.

I've been that shadow, too—
lurking.
Too afraid to knock,
too proud to beg.
But here, now,
I've opened the door.

Yes.
You are invited in.

Not to my bed,
but to my sanctum.
My hollows.
My hearth.

Here, there is no need to pretend.
You can drop your seductions
and your sharp, practiced lines.
Let your accent thicken.
Let your fear stutter.
Let your breath go uneven.

I do not want the polished version.
I want the creature you hide

beneath layers of longing.

I want to laugh with your demons.
I want to dance with your doubts.
I want to kiss the part of you
that still doesn't believe
it's worthy of being seen.

So come—
step beyond the myth.
Not every invitation ends in blood.
Many end in belonging.

And I?
I've lit the candles.
I've unlocked the doors.
I've written this with your name
etched between every line.

All that's left
is your knock.

## Forest Green

Deep in this forest green,
where time stands still,
two Black bodies perform
an intricate dance; one of sweet seduction,
in a language unspoken.

I see you. You see me.
But we never speak—
maybe too shy
to name what we seek,
or too ashamed of the very act
we came here to do.

You hid beneath the canopy,
past the old amphitheater trail,
stalking, watching,
drawn to pursuit of me—
predator and prey
blurring in the breath between us.

But I know you're there.
So I wait, half-shadow, half-invitation,
nested in the hush of Fort DuPont.

Still, it doesn't stop us.

We bite the forbidden fruit
of this sacred green,
taste its sweet nectar—
the kind you can't grow at home,
can't bottle, can't confess.

And maybe that's why
we keep coming back here.

Deeper. Still deeper.

Hands whisper along bark-stained hips,
mouths grazing like breeze on wet leaves.
Your breath—
a sermon in my ear.
My gasp—
a prayer pressed to your shoulder.
We praise without words,
worship with grind and grip.

You taste like sweat and secrecy.
I bloom in the heat of your grip.
And still—you never ask for my name.

And if you did,
I would tell you it was Jay,
knowing I lied
just to save face.

Just the body.
Just the moment.
Just the craving.

The earth shifts beneath us.
Mosquitoes bear witness.
Branches bend in time
with our rhythm.
Nature don't judge,
she only records.

When it's all over,
we vanish—
like mist,
like myth,
like the men who know how to find one another
beneath thick trees
off of Minnesota and Alabama,
where the woods remember more
than we're willing to admit.
Where the ground still hums
with every secret we never speak aloud.

## The Space Between

You stood too close
for a nigga tryin' not to fuck.
That wasn't just a glance,
that was a choice.
To not touch. To not say.
To let the moment sit there and sweat.

Your breath hit my neck
like you forgot where you were—
like maybe you thought I wouldn't notice
how you looked at me like a question
you wanted me to answer.

But I held it.
Held myself.
Because I've been there before—
burned myself trying to love someone
still too scared to admit
he likes the heat.

You looked at me like you've already fucked me.
Like you've played it out in your head,
hands on ass,
mouth on my neck, messy sheets,
name slipping out your throat
like something holy.

But then you said *what's up*
like it meant nothing,
just a head nod.
Like your pupils weren't screaming
what your mouth couldn't say.

You stood tense as a prayer,
hard as guilt,
quiet as shame.

And I was ready.
I would've taken you right there,
not for sex,
but for the surrender.
I wanted the way you melt
when no one's watching.
The way your voice drops
when you stop pretending.

But you tucked it in.
Fixed your collar.
Smirked like this wasn't shit.
Walked out like you hadn't just stood
ten inches away
from something real.
Something dangerous.

And I let you because
I know what it costs
to fuck someone
who ain't ready to look in the mirror after.
Not because I'm scared.

You don't know this,
but I've written you in every room
we didn't touch.
Every bar. Every train.
Every late-night that smelled like maybe.

You'll keep pretending it didn't happen.
And I'll stop pretending I needed it to.

You wanted me—
and I wanted something true.

But this?
Was just the space between.

---

## Jacks Grinder Bio

Rooted in Ogun, but I still reach.
Sag rising, Libra sun, Pisces moon—
balanced chaos in flesh.
So yes, I want to be held, I want to be heard—
but touch me wrong and I'll vanish like smoke.

5'11.
Weight shifts with the weather.
Body type? Blessed by both hunger and healing.
Ethnicity? Soul Food.
Position? Depends on the rhythm, the room,
and if you washed your sheets or your sins.

Looking For: Respect, release, maybe a ride.

Tribe: Ancestors. Don't ask again.

Distance:
253 feet away.
Still too far for real connection.
Too close for you to lie and me not feel it.

Curious?
Why you asking like I ain't layered—
like I'm a menu not a man?
I'm into taking my time till time forgets we were strangers.
Into thighs and theology,
mirror sex and moonlight rituals.
Into back rubs that end in revelations,
morning-after meals and mid-spell kisses.
I'm into whoever asks better questions.

Bio (Real Talk):
I'm not here to decode your "Sup."
I don't do headless profiles—
unless it's a metaphor for ego death.
Don't call yourself "real" if you ghost by sunrise.
Don't call yourself "spiritual" if your ancestors wouldn't recognize you.

---

I light candles before I bust,
pray after,
breathe between bodies, remembering mine.
Balance chakras between sessions.

Favorites:
Late-night playlists with dirty lyrics and deeper meaning.
The weight of a man's voice when he says I got you.
That moment we laugh mid-stroke—
because something beautiful slipped out.

Dislikes:
The myth that softness expires with age.
Being asked "What you looking for?" by people not ready to be found.
"NSA" energy from souls who want me to hold them like secrets
but won't even say their real name.

Intentions:
I'm not building a situationship with someone
who can't sit in silence.
If you can't match my breath,
you can't touch my body.
If your presence don't hum in my nervous system—
keep scrolling.

Final Line:
Yes, I'm looking.
I'm looking for recognition,
a familiar pull—
something that makes the noise go quiet.
But not just a good time.

So if you feel that—
come correct.
And maybe, just maybe,
I'll let you really see me.

Or not.

## Maybe

Maybe I should've known when silence came first—
as absence, not as peace.
The kind that sits in your chest
when you're waiting for a name to mean something
never fully said out loud.

We met on a maybe,
kissed like a promise,
but loved like a ghost story.
Here one moment,
gone the next—
haunted, never held.

You said, "I'm scared
of falling in love with you."
But I think you were more scared
of what loving me could be—
a present of...
no longer hiding behind pretty words
that couldn't hold weight.

Some people would rather engage an algorithm
than engage another's rhythm.
Easier to swipe than sync.
Easier to type "I miss you"
than show up when it matters.
They craved connection,
then run from communion.
And I?
I was offering my WiFi password
to someone still looking for a signal.

I gave grace like water,
but even oceans know when to recede.

And, this is not a goodbye laced with bitterness,
but a release—
of all the *almosts* I held like certainties.
Of all the red flags I folded into rose petals.
Of all the longing that belonged more to my childhood
than to you.

Maybe you'll figure it out.
Maybe I will too.
But this time,
I'm not waiting on a *maybe*
to love me like a *yes*.

## It's Ok...It's Safe

One of the last things I asked my brother was,
"How are you taking care of you?"
And it sat in the silence,
like a question he'd never been taught how to answer.

We, the sons of steel-spined mamas
and soft-spoken daddies who held pain in their palms,
were told early:
Protect. Provide. Push through.
And never cry where someone could see the break.

So we learned to bottle.
To silence the shaking.
To worship busy hands
and call our exhaustion an offering.
And when it cracked—
we patched it with women, with weed, with withdrawal,
or whatever kept the world from noticing the fall.

I'm no judging, fam.
I was there too.
I've laid down in arms
just to avoid laying down the truth.

But then one day, I cracked in a quiet room—
no crowd, no script, just me and truth.
And the sister across from me didn't flinch
when my voice shook,
didn't rush me when I had no name for this pain.

She just said,
*Let's start here.*
And for the first time, I did.

Not for them.
Not for the strength I thought I had to perform.
But for the little boy in me
who got left behind trying to be the man too soon.

---

Therapy didn't save me.
It gave me space to save myself.

To name my grief.
To speak my fear.
To say "I'm tired" without shame.
To let the tears come
and not question if I was a man after.

I felt my ancestors in that silence too.
(Not judging, just watching.):
Men who swallowed rage
so I could spit the truth.
Men who died with their clenched fists
and hearts aching
so I could unclench mine
and finally start shaking—
and still live.

I heard them hum in my chest like loud bass,
like *You ain't weak, nephew.*
*You just the first with a safe enough space.*

So, brothers—
if you're hearing this;
if your days get heavy
and your nights fall long,
if you've been tired of being tired
but can't name where it's coming from—

Let this be your reminder:
You're not alone.
You're not broken.
Healing is not a betrayal of your strength.

You don't have to be perfect.
You don't have to push through everything alone.
There is no race.
No mask required.

Remember to breathe,
remember to rest,
and know just showing up is enough.

Your softness is sacred.
Your tears are testimony.
And every time you choose to heal,
you're not just saving yourself—
you're freeing somebody else.

## When You Come Back to Visit....Ma

You always asked two things when we talked on the phone —
"Have you been to the doctor?" and "When last you cooked at home?"
And even now in spirit, when you come around slow,
it's the same tone, same pause—like you already know.

I hear you in the skillet, in the pop of hot grease,
when the seasoning hits just right and the flavors find peace.
Ma, I'm still chasing your smothered shrimp,
but it's not just taste — it's your soul put in it.

I remember you watching us eat like that was your prize.
It was weird back then — but we knew why.
When you said, "Y'all go ahead," we felt the cue—
you were tasting joy through every chew.

And Lord knows, you were stubborn as fire,
never backed down, never tired to yell.
Asking the same questions ten different ways—
not nosy, just loving through a sideways gaze.

You didn't play about us, your kids.
You gave what you had and kept nothing hid.
You could be loud when silence would do,
and it was never to shame—just to cut through.

Even when you didn't get all my ways,
you stood like a wall, unfazed by the maze.
Didn't need details to love me whole.
You said I was your baby—and that fed my soul.

You were my biggest cheerleader when storms rolled in,
even when life wore your edges thin.
You saw my pen before I could speak.
Said, "Just write it down, I need to see something this week."

And when I'd get quiet, lost in my head,
you'd check me quick with the words you said,

"Why are you letting the books outdo you?
You smart enough to outdo the books."

That line still rings when I doubt my page—
like you blessed me early with a writer's stage.
You knew my shine before I could see—
like brilliance was baked into you and me.

You wrote too—just not out loud.
Tucked your truth under grief and clouds.
Now I write in double, echoing your sound,
my voice braided with the strength you found.

I still find you in undone pots,
in over-seasoned meals and scattered thoughts.
Some days, I don't speak at all—
and wonder if that silence is you, standing tall.

You come by quiet, with no real sign—
in Liz Taylor's scent or Glade's faint line.
Before the pot boils or a blank page wins,
I feel you there, whispering me in.

Today was perfect for fishing and sun.
You would've laughed at how bad I'd done.
Teased me good, then cursed the fish—
when your line stayed dry and missed its wish.

But it was never about the fish we lost—
just time we shared, no matter the cost.
Your love was time, cast out and reeled—
no bait needed, just what we feel.

If you're listening: yes, I've gone.
No, they ain't cured me, but I'm holding on.
I'm whole in ways I can't explain—
and still, your love runs through my veins.

And yes—I cooked. Took my time.
Made your shrimp, your rhythm, your rhyme.

Waited till they took that bite—
watched them grin like your spirit lit the night.

And Ma...it was good.
Just like you always said it would.

I'm still your baby. Still dancing your flame,
still hearing your cheers when I whisper my name.
One day I'll make that banana pudding right—
vanilla wafers stacked, cool whip light.
I'll eat it slow and call it a win.
And know that you'd be smiling within.

## Catchin' Up...

### ...with my Sisiter

Girl,
you still rockin' them Dumbo ears?
I swear they caught more gossip than the radio.
Used to twitch when Mama talked slick
two rooms over.
We hold in a laugh
'til your tank hissed
and gave us away.

I can still hear that sound—
oxygen and attitude,
like God was whisperin'
*not yet*
every time you exhaled.

You said that once
with a smirk that softened the truth.
And I laughed—
because even with tubes in your arm,
you still sounded like Big Sis,
still rolled your eyes
when I asked too many questions.

I remember you say,
*Don't let the sickness fool you.*
And you meant it.
Even with that tube under your nose,
you had enough spirit to check all of us
with one eyebrow.

I miss that.
I miss you.

But I don't want to write about IV drips.
I want to write about the way you listened.
Like the world would pause

just to hear what I had to say.
Like I mattered—
even when I didn't know how to speak yet.

You be proud though—
I'm talkin' more now.
Writin' poems.
Still tryin' to figure this love thing out
without makin' it hurt so much.
And your cats?
Yeah... they still think they run the place.

That daughter of yours?
Whew.
You raised her right.
Strong mind, stronger will—
she got your fire
and your don't-play-that tone.
She's a full-grown woman now,
the kind of woman you were shaping
even when you were running on fumes.

You'd love her husband—
real solid.
Respects her, honors her,
lets her be as bold as she was born to be.
They got three little ones now.
Yep—
you're a grandma, sis.
And guess what?
They got your ears.
Big, beautiful, all-heaing ears.
Like maybe God wanted your spirit
to keep catching every whisper
this family needs.

Sometimes I wonder
if you visit them when I'm not looking.
When they stare off at nothing,
or curl up like they know somethin' I don't.

You were always patient with me.
Even when I didn't know what I needed.
You let me ramble.
Let me cry.
Told me the truth
with sugar on it—
but not too much.

There were days I'd crash on your couch,
like the whole world had worn me out.
But your peace wrapped around me
like a favorite blanket.
To this day, I'm still tryna build my home
with your same kind of quiet love.

So let me tell you something now:
You weren't just the sick one.
You were the strong one.
The real one.
The one who made peace feel like home.

Some days I still reach for the phone.
Forget for a second that
you don't answer that way anymore.

But I feel you.
In the quiet.
In the hiss of steam from the kettle.
In the pause between my own breaths
when I finally slow down enough to listen.

You never left me.
You just switched how you show up.
And I'm still catching up.

## Parallel Prayer:

### For my Brother

I never questioned if you loved me,
but *damn*, I wish you hugged me.
Not just with words or holy fire,
but with the arms of a flawed messiah.

You wore the cloth, I wore the storm,
you preached the word, I wrote my form.
Same God, different roads we took;
you had a Bible, I had a notebook.

You were the middle, I was the end,
the little brother trying to pretend
that silence meant peace, that distance was fine,
but it was just pain dressed in time.

Mama's gone, and Sis is too,
and now I grieve the ghost of you.
Not just the man, but the *might-have-been*,
the brother I longed for beneath your skin.

We cooked our meals, watched old shows,
but never let our soft sides show.
Your love was quiet, proud, devout;
mine was loud, and full of doubt.

You raised four kids—left pieces of you
in their every smile, in all they do.
Your son? He mirrors all your light,
your fire, your temper, your sacred fight.

Your girls? Man, they lit your sky.
Especially the youngest, with your wise-guy eyes.
And your wife... she was your twin in truth,
your mirror, your muse, your living proof.

The way she looked at you—soft and sure,
the kind of love that could endure

---

the Sunday suits, the hospital nights,
the backseat prayers, the motorbike flights.

She held you down and lifted you high,
kissed your wounds, praised your why.
If love is real, y'all made it clear—
through every joy, and every tear.

But me? I walk a softer line,
no pulpit calls, no suits, no sign.
I talk to God through trees and sky,
in rustling leaves and moonlight high.

I've prayed beneath the live oak tree,
found peace where rivers speak to me.
No choir songs, but crickets sing
and I feel grace in everything.

Now you rest, and I remain
the last of three, the echo of pain.
But I'll stand tall where you once stood,
watching over your girls, like a brother should.

I'll check on Daddy, ease his sigh,
and tell your son it's okay to cry.
I'll leave the door cracked for the daughter you missed,
and send her grace in every twist.

You rode with purpose, man of steel;
you lived your truth, you kept it real.
And I'll live mine, no robe, no choir,
just ink and breath, and soul on fire.

So if you hear this on the other side,
between the clouds, beneath the tide,
know I still love you, loud and true,
and I'm becoming a better man... because of you.

## The Spark in My Father

*...This is for you*

He never had to raise his voice
for a room to listen.
Daddy speaks like the wind...
soft, steady,
but you feel it when it moves through you.

He could fix anything.
Didn't matter if it was wood, wire, or engine—
his hands knew how to translate broken things
back into something useful.
Beautiful, even.

People took advantage of that—
that open-door kindness,
that "I'll help if I can" spirit.
He never said much about it.
Just shrugged, smiled,
and got back to work.

Sometimes I think
the world never gave him
the love his hands deserved.

But there's a spark in him
a little glint behind his quiet.
You'll miss it if you're not paying attention.
It shows up when he talks about the stars,
or how to measure twice, cut once,
or why trees lean the way they do in storms.

Now, I see pieces of you in me.
The way I love trees more than cities.
The way I explain chaos like it's a constellation—
nonsensical to most,
but perfectly patterned in my head.

---

I catch myself in moments
where your spirit shows up:
when I take something apart just to understand it,
when I fix something
no one else noticed was broken.
When I disappear for a while
but still show up when it counts.

You never asked for attention.
You let your work speak.
And somehow,
it always knew what to say.

You're not a man of many words,
but the ones you keep have weight.
And even when I didn't always understand you,
I always saw the spark.

So no,
you're not perfect
but you're one of the first men I learned to watch closely.
Not only for what you'd say,
but also how you moved through this world
with calloused hands and unspoken hope.
You taught me that silence
can be sacred,
that kindness doesn't need a witness
to be real.
And even now
when I measure the men I want to be,
I still trace the lines
back to you.

## God Never Said Sorry

### A Letter to the Almighty

You said *You would never leave or forsake me.*
Though, I see Your presence everywhere—
You never noticed mine.
I was born into a house already cracking,
right when my father started slipping.
I hear the stories of how life used to be—
family trips and laughter.
Joy that vanished the moment I arrived.
Like I was the storm they wouldn't name.

You let my mother survive things no woman should.
I was nine, maybe twelve,
hearing whispers I wasn't meant to hear,
watching her carry pain like a second spine.
I wanted to help.
But I was too young.
And You—too silent.

You allowed my father to seek his therapy
through bottles and pipes.
He hid his pain of being forgotten
in the clouds I guessed were too low for You to reach.

God, look what that did to me!
I learned to love in whispers,
to hide my softness behind smirk and bass.
I wore shame like cologne—
heavy enough to announce my arrival
before anyone could get close.

I prayed the gay out of me—
begged for You to make me anything
but what made men disappear.
Nights, I traced halos around my reflection,
draw wings across my shoulder blades,
wondering if even angels

ever felt my kind of loneliness.

I kept giving myself away
like communion—
hoping someone might taste me
and call it holy.

But the silence stayed.
And I mistook it for punishment.
For proof that I was unworthy
of Your attention.

You watched my sister,
all patience and light,
fight lupus like she owed You something.
She was kind even when her body wasn't.
Always more grace than complaint.
And still, You let her go.

You gave my brother secrets too heavy to name.
He grieved things out loud by staying quiet.
His love came in sideward glances and quick nods, not hugs.
He held his pain in his chest so close and sacred.
I never knew how to reach him.
I still don't.

Even in church, where they swore You lived,
I never found You.
I found noise. Rules.
Promises translated by preachers
into lives that never looked like mine.
I believed Your Word. Quoted it!
Waited for the peace they said would come.
But I got stillness
that felt more like absence than presence.

I asked You why I am the way I am.
Why I felt like a ghost even when I was kissed.
Why touch became a language I spoke just to feel seen.
Why I gave myself away hoping someone might finally stay.

---

I never got an answer.

Sometimes I picture You standing with arms folded—
watching me drown with that quiet look that says,
*Figure it out.*
No rescue.
No instructions.
A divine shrug dressed as sovereignty.

Maybe this is blasphemy.
Maybe it's clarity.
But I didn't need a miracle.
I needed mercy.
I didn't need prophecy.
I needed presence.
A whisper.
A shoulder.
A God who saw the child behind the grown-man body and said:
"You didn't deserve any of that.
I'm sorry."

## .....But I Was Here

*His Response*

> *Can you hear me? I was there.*
> *Maybe you couldn't—not with the noise life blasted your way,*
> *tearing your eardrumsthe same way your heart tore.*

*They told you I was only thunder,*
*but I lived in your silence.*
*In the breath you held*
*so your mother wouldn't hear you cry.*
*In the pause between "I'm fine" and falling apart.*

*How do you think you got out of bed some mornings?*
*That wasn't just willpower.*
*That was Me, quiet in your spine.*
*In your second wind.*
*In the sigh that said, not again... but okay.*

*Even when you said*
*I never said sorry—*
*I didn't flinch. I just waited.*
*Waited for you to finish.*
*Waited to be seen.*

*Over and over, I stayed.*
*Not outside of you but within you.*
*You didn't see Me in grief,*
*but I was there—*
*in the hands that helped you stand back up,*
*in the pen you picked up*
*when the pain needed somewhere to live.*

*D*on't think I missed your mother's cries,
or your father slipping away
into the hush of high and hollow.
You were born into their unraveling.
They couldn't fix it, but I stayed.
And when you held their pain,
I held you.

*O*ver time, you mistook My silence for absence.
But I wasn't gone.
I was learning to speak your language—
stillness...poems.
Half-finished prayers scribbled in the dark.

*R*emember your sister's laugh?
Her light? Her grace even when her body betrayed her?
That was Me, too.
Reaching through her smile
to tell you not everything dies the moment it hurts.

*E*ven your brother—cold as he seemed—
carried grief he never named.
He held secrets in his chest
like stones wrapped in cloth.
He loved you,
just not in words.
That love was Me Too.

*Maybe...you were embarrassed of me.*
*You couldn't call me by my name.*
*Maybe you didn't know it.*
*Should I remind you?*

*They said I was too soft.*
*So you stopped calling Me.*
*So I stopped trying to be loud.*
*I curled small. Just like you.*
*And every time you cried alone,*
*I did too.*

*Every bruise you took*
*just to feel wanted—*
*I never blamed you.*
*I wanted to be held too.*
*I just didn't know how to ask.*

*Don't blame yourself for needing touch.*
*That was Me—aching with you,*
*hiding in your poems,*
*in quiet victories,*
*in bruises you mistook for love.*

*Down here,*
*in your most fragile moments,*
*I was always gathering the pieces*
*you kept throwing away.*

*You saw Me again last night.*
*In the mirror.*
*And for the first time,*
*you didn't look away.*
*You named Me.*
*And I answered.*

*Then you look in the mirror...*

*T*his...
*this is what becoming looks like.*
*Not perfect.*
*But whole.*

*H*ow powerful you are
*now that you've stopped splitting.*
*Now that the Boy and the God*
*can sit at the same table*
*without fear.*

*E*very version of you still lives here.
*The weeping child.*
*The reckless lover.*
*The one who asked why—*
*and the one who finally answered.*

*O*ver and over again,
*you kept choosing life.*
*Even when it didn't choose you back.*

*You don't have to find Me anymore.*
*You became Me.*
*And I never left.*

---

# WE'RE GOING

## The Mirror Knows

When I was twelve, I stood in the mirror—
shirtless, by chance.
I saw a man trying to break through
collarbones and curiosity,
a flicker of a jawline,
a question in his chest.

Now, I stand half-naked
in front of that same glass,
waiting for him to show up again.
Because I've been looking for him—
in barbershop banter thick with laughter and lies,
in fatherless prayers,
in the flex of men walking by
like they know something I don't.

I watched men with muscles like armor,
veins mapping their arms like rivers
I didn't know how to cross.
I thought manhood meant less softness,
more sweat,
more spit in your laugh,
more steel in your step.

I thought softness was a symptom.
Thought loving the way another man carried his weight
meant I was broken—
or at least bent
in ways I couldn't explain.

But I didn't want their bodies.
I wanted their belonging.
Wanted to be let into that quiet language—
the nod, the clasped handshake,
the unspoken rhythm of being enough
without having to say it.

So I practiced in secret.
Lowered my voice in the hallway.

---

Walked slower, like I wasn't rushing
to find myself.

Then one day, I stopped performing.
Let my shoulders drop.
Let my laugh come out high and unbothered.
Let my softness speak
without apology in its mouth.

I found strength in stillness—
in lighting incense instead of lifting weight,
in writing what I couldn't say out loud,
in letting myself cry
without waiting for the shower to run.

I started loving my body,
not for what it could hold up,
but for how it held me—
steady when nothing else did.
For how it carried twelve-year-old me
through rooms too sharp for his softness,
and still made it here.

I stopped chasing manhood like a medal
and started honoring it like a mirror—
not something I had to wear,
but something I was.

And now,
I stand before the mirror, half-naked—
not waiting,
but witnessing.

I smile at the man I've become:
the voice that doesn't shake,
the heart that still does.
The softness wrapped in spine,
the boy who didn't break.

I am the man I was looking for—
the one who stayed,

———————————

who learned that love
doesn't mean less feeling,
it means more permission.

I trace the line from then to now,
and there he is—
that twelve-year-old boy
still peeking through the collarbones.

So I nod.
So he knows.
We made it.

## Red Line Stop

What happens to a dream when realized?

Does it bloom—
bloom like a fresh rose in May?
Petals wide, perfume spilling,
making the whole block turn their head your way?

Or does it haunt—
haunt like a ghost of what could have been,
a shadow of your own hands
reaching for something they already hold?

Does it call to the hungry,
call them close with the smell of something sweet—
a plate so pretty you forget it's just for looking?

Maybe it waits—
waits in the corner like a song nobody plays,
aching for a needle to drop,
aching to be heard.

Or does it sour—
turn bitter on the tongue,
like sugar left too long in the rain—
sweet once,
but now crumbling into nothing?

## Father of The Cosmic Beat

I am the Father of the Cosmic Beat.
Not just a DJ—I conjure heat.
I don't spin records. I bend the air.
Fade into rhythm. Reappear as prayer.

Not loud, but steady. Not seen, but known.
Like a drum carved deep into ancestral bone.
A nod. A tilt. My hands in the sound—
blessing this temple with no one around.

I don't drop the beat; I guard the flame.
I hold the space. I own the claim.
The pulse. The anchor. The soul's design.
The sacred hush between the lines.

Then she arrives; not echo, but sun.
The Black Goddess. The chosen one.
Her hips in crescent, her skin in sway,
hair braided with yesterday's sacred clay.

She don't need lights. She is the shine.
She dances in silence and calls it divine.
When she moves, the spirit hums—
like church bells beatin' house drums.

The dancers? Our children. Spirit-fed.
Spinning truth on rubber tread.
They dip like water, rise like steam—
the body remembering its dream.

There's a boy catching rhythm like breath for the first.
A woman breaking free from the church.
An elder whose knees forgot the pace—
but his shoulders still carry the bass.

And when she twirls? That ain't for show.
She's cleansing shame from head to toe.
Every stomp is a gospel line.

Every whine rewinds the spine.

I just keep it steady, no tricks, no boast—
a safe place for her to land the ghost.
That's my offering. That's my role.
The Father of the Beat. The keeper of soul.

There's no climax—just becoming.
The memory of drumming, the rhythm still humming.
No need for claps. Just breath, just nod—
just sweat-born hallelujahs to God.

I am the Divine. Not loud, not grand—
Rooted like truth in a griot's pause,
Held like breath before a testimony.
I'm not your savior. I'm your base.
The scaffold holding sacred space.

And she...
She is fire, and flesh, and flow.
The beat in the bones. The glow you know.
We don't perform. We call it back.
Each drop a flame, each breath a track.

We raise the altar. We spin the set.
And in that space? Our people sweat.
They rise again. They find their feet.
To the rhythm I hold—

I am the Father of the Cosmic Beat.

## Convenience

It was all fine and dandy
when I was just a convenience.
Easy access to me, no boundary.
felt so good... naturally.
You and me in sweet harmony.
But every convenience has a fee,
and access to me incurred a cost.

It requires attention
met with intention.
Love without condition.
A space that actually feels safe.

Now I'm out of place—
a thief among saints.

But we were just playing for the moment.
Being everything in that moment—
lovers and friends...
well, more lover than friend.
Not really a lover,
just a nigga you fuck to the end.
Only when you're ready again.
And only at your convenience.

And I allowed it.
Because I wanted it—
I wanted you.
Didn't matter how bare I was—
I found a way to feel whole,
hoping you'd fill this hole.
And you did...
with your carnal nature.
And I was ad-dic-ted.

My heart, I was willing to wager—
but only at your convenience.

---

I gave freely.
No concern of supply.
You had the demand—
and I always complied.
You called—I ran and obeyed.
You were Simon.
And I definitely can.
Only at your convenient command.

No regard for my deep within—
just as long as I could fit in.
But I could'nt just blend in.
Not anymore. I'll be settling
for the illusion of a life
too full of strife.

No emotional check-ins.
No "how your day been's."
Just endless Netflix and chill-ins.

Sigh...This is boring.
I want something I can pour my soul in—
not just feel swollen.

Is that such an inconvenience?
Have I asked for too much?
Did I turn you away
with my need for touch?

Could you like me enough
to be more than a fuck?
Or must I keep shrinking
into something more convenient?

Nah...Fuck that.

My convenience costs.
Access to me is no longer free.
And the fee?
Is love...unconditionally.

## Treason Season

I'm okay that you left—
for reasons you delivered
like the hook of a song
you never intended to finish.

Maybe it made sense
in your verse.
But I was singing harmony,
and you'd already picked a solo stage.

I had to divest—
peel myself off your rhythm
like a skipped track
on the album I was trying to believe in.

This ain't where you'll find me.
No reruns.
No replays.
No looking back
at the garden you swore wasn't growing.

You called it "not enough."
Said I was "no longer beneficial,"
like I was a prelude
you outgrew
when the beat changed.

You went searching for rare finds—
a cleaner mix,
a glossier track,
someone whose love don't crack
under pressure.

But what is it you're really chasing?
A high without the harmony?
A melody that don't ask questions?

---

You're entitled to your season.
And everything has a season.
But this?
This felt like treason.

Like when someone says, "care for me, care for me,"
but they're halfway out the door.
Like a promise whispered slow and warm
that never makes it past the night.
Not enough to stay.
Not enough to build.

And me?
I was doing just fine
until your silence arrived
like a bridge I couldn't cross.
You left with verses unfinished,
and I was still stuck
writing hooks
around your absence.

But still—
I rise like vinyl.
Scratched,
but soulful.
Worn,
but still worth the spin.

Don't play me
unless you're ready to listen
all the way through.

## Where The Forest Meet The Storm

I wasn't made to play it safe.
I was made to move like mist—
quiet in my arrival,
loud in what I leave behind.

I am the calm
and the storm that follows.

I walk into a room
and people feel something shift—
like incense before the sermon,
like heat before the rain.
Like a hush that ain't fear—
it's reverence.

I've been doubted in rooms where I outshined them.
Felt stupid next to people I outgrew.
Sat on panels, stages, mics,
thinking, maybe I snuck in here by accident.
But the truth is—
I didn't sneak.
I summoned.

They think resilience is strength.
But mine is silence sharpened over time.
A soft "no" that feels like a closed door.
A smile that don't beg for permission.
A voice that don't rise—
it pulls you under.

I am the calm
and the storm that follows.

Only time will tell
what all this pressure's for.
But I already know how to turn weight into rhythm,
loneliness into lighting,
awkwardness into intimacy,

and delay into a divine slow burn.

I've kissed men
like they were the only language I spoke.
And prayed after,
not out of shame—
but to say thank you
for a body that still wants to feel.
Still wants to love,
even after love let me bleed on the floor
and dance through it like it was mine.

I've danced with ghosts
and told them,
"Y'all can stay if you dance with me."
I've offered up my triggers
as turntables,
my pain as percussion,
my voice as vinyl.

I don't spin songs.
I spin spirit.

I am the calm
and the storm that follows.

I've walked through forests
not for peace,
but for conversation.
I like when the wind talks back.
I like when the trees don't ask questions.
I like when I disappear into the green
and come out more myself
than the world lets me be.

The ocean?
That's where I saw her—
dancing in a hurricane,
barefoot, unbothered.

Said, "Child, if they don't see your power,
blind them with movement."

I don't need a stage.
I am the performance.
I am the altar.
I am the spell.
A mixtape of spirit and survival.
A body baptized in its own return.

Everybody wants to clean a clean toilet.
Nobody wants to touch what's already been used.
But baby—
I've scrubbed myself down to soul
and still had the nerve to shine.

I am the calm
and the storm that follows.

You want to know who I am?

I'm what the storm leaves behind
when it's done being polite.
I'm the remix of survival.
The groove in grief.
The echo that don't fade.
The hush before the holy.

I'm not safe.
I'm sacred.
I'm not asking for time—
I'm telling it:

Watch me.

I came here with no map—
but I still brought my tools.

I am the calm
and the storm that follows.

## *Still, I Want To Try*

I've let men
break me open like communion bread.
Took my body like sacrament,
but never stayed for the benediction.
Said amen with their zippers
and disappeared like smoke.

> But you—
> you don't eat and run.
> You sit with me after the ache.
> You ask about my day
> while your fingertips still smell like last night.
> And I don't know what to do with that.

I've mistaken rhythm for romance.
Good dick for good intentions.
Whispers for commitment.
I've been the soft landing
for men in freefall.

> But your weight feels different.
> Not like falling,
> more like planting.
> Like you're building a home
> and I might be the land.

I've been ghosted so hard
I almost believed I was a myth.
A brief fantasy.
A body caught between algorithms and appetite.
A warm place to rest,
not a name you remember.

> But you remember.
> Even the things I tried to forget.
> You say my full name
> like a spell
> you want to cast slowly.

Nobody's supposed to be here—
and yet...
you're still in my chest
like bassline and regret.
Nobody's supposed to be here—
but your voice feels like
a second chance at breath.

I know this song.
I've danced to it before.
In kitchens, in bedrooms,
on knees.
The part where love shows up
just to remind me
what I still can't hold.

But what if this time
isn't a remix of my pain?
What if your kiss
ain't just choreography
to distract me from leaving again?

I'm scared.
Scared of who I become
when I believe someone wants me
without a disclaimer.
And in the morning after,
I wait for the phone to buzz.
My heart stops—
because it might be you.
But it sinks
when it's not.

Still, I play it cool.
Tell myself it's nothing.
That I'm not waiting.
That I'm not watching the screen
like it owes me closure.

But truth is,
I want to text you:
"I want to see you again."
And not mean just for the night.
I want to stop auditioning for survival.
Want to let your hands
be a stage I don't have to perform on.

I'm learning to fall in love with you.
Not because you're hard to love—
but because I'm still learning
to love myself
in the presence
of someone who stays.

## I Heard A Love Poem Tonight

I heard a love poem tonight,
and it made me think of you.
But I don't remember how it went.
If I could paraphrase,
it went something like this:

Love arrives
like a thief with soft feet.
Not to steal,
but to place things
inside you
you'll never remove.

It moves like water—
sometimes a kiss,
sometimes a flood.
Sometimes a hand on your thigh
when you're halfway through a story
you didn't think mattered.

I heard a love poem tonight,
and tried to paraphrase it again
in the shower,
in the car,
in the pause before sleep.
But every version sounded
more like us
than the poet who wrote it.

It said love is the breath
between moans.
The weight of a gaze
that makes you forget
what you were ashamed of.

And I thought about
your hands—
how they opened me

like scripture.
No demand,
just discovery.
Like you were trying
to read me aloud
in the right language.

It said love shows up
in the things we forget—
the way someone lifts your shirt
like peeling fruit,
or how their silence
can feel like applause
after you've given everything
but still aren't chosen.

I remembered
how we didn't need music.
Just the creak of the bed,
our rhythm—unrushed.
You moved like you worshipped before,
but never like this.

I heard a love poem tonight,
and wondered if I ever really forgot it—
or if the truth just needed
your name
to rise.

The poem said love
isn't always loud,
but it's always felt.
In the way you held my jaw
after kissing it raw.
In the way you said "you good?"
and meant it
in the deepest part of your voice.

It said love should feel like home.
And I swear—
when your breath met my spine,
I believed I became the house.
the door an the key.
The welcome mat you never wiped your feet on,
because I never you'll never soiled me.

Maybe I was never quoting anyone.
Maybe we were the lines.
Maybe this is how love writes itself—
out loud,
in bodies,
with no title,
no author but touch.

I heard a love poem tonight.
But maybe...
this is how it went.

## Astronomy of Us

We trace each other's trauma
like constellations—
not to relive the burn,
but to chart new worlds
in the nebula that remains.

You ask me where it hurts,
and I don't flinch.
I point to dying stars
still sending their light—
late, but faithful.

You touch me
like you've studied the night,
learned its language,
still believe in the sequel
written in the dark.

Like you've kissed the ghosts
and called them comets,
watched them return every few years
just to prove the sky remembers.

You know love isn't light.
It's fusion—
heat made from gravity and surrender,
forged in collapse and carried anyway.

You ask what I'm into—
and I don't say bodies.
I say stillness...lunar quiet,
being held like atmosphere,
not convenience.
I say showing up in orbit—
steady, slow,
Tuesday morning gravity.
Not in meteoric gestures.

And when you whisper,
"You feel like home,"
I almost say it back—
almost let the words rise
without choking on gravity.

Instead, I just breathe.
I hesitate.
I draft escape routes
when you linger too long in my orbit.
I keep a laugh on standby
to mask the flare of fear,
still hear echoes from men
who praised my fire
but fled when it dimmed.

But you—
you pull steady.
Not a chase.
Not a snare.
Just presence—
the kind even gods envy.
A gravity that hums,
not demands.

You name constellations
in the scars I hid.
You make the silence sing again.

And I don't know if this is real
or the sky is lying again,
Am I just a planet
trying to love a comet
who always burns too bright,
too fast?

But you don't scorch.
You simmer—
an eclipse of calm and wonder.

Tonight,
I let you draw galaxies on my back
with your fingers—
slow, deliberate,
like you know
every crater holds a psalm.

We don't rush.
We don't pretend.

So if this is a myth,
let me believe it anyway.
Let me stand in this starlight
a little longer—
not searching for omens,
but finally choosing
to be seen.

Because maybe love
isn't written in stars,
but in the spaces we make.

*We're Gone*

What if, one morning,
we were just... gone?

No smoke. No spark.
Just dust where divinity used to dance.
Just silence—
that stubborn kind
you feel in your teeth.

The porch swing still swings,
but the air forgot the smell of hot combs and high notes.
No grease-stained wisdom on the stoop,
no "baby, you eat yet?"
just wind
where welcome used to be.

No cookouts. No cousin nicknames.
No little girls with barrettes
clicking like Morse code joy.
No barbershop baptism.
No church fan ministry.
No "you got this"
in hoop earrings and hurricane faith.

We didn't leave.
We ascended.
Took our tambourines and tenderness with us.
Took our side-eyes and second lines.
Took the moonwalk, the body roll,
the hush before a testimony,
and the "amen" that made the roof lift.

Gone.

Left you with rhythm, but no roots.
Fashion, but no flavor.

A tongue, but no taste.

Your mirrors now don't curve.
Your TikToks glitch.
Your denim don't sit right.
Your anthem got no bass.

The world scrolls on,
but the vibe got gentrified.
The streets stay paved—
but nobody praise-dances on the corners.

We weren't erased.
We just stopped showing up
to places that never learned how to see us.

Our names still echo in the steam.
Our laughter still loops in the vinyl.
Our halos hang from every streetlight
you replaced with LED.

What if the moon
lost just enough light
to make lovers doubt themselves?
What if joy felt illegal—
without a soundtrack?

Would you notice
the hole in the harmony?
The missing sugar in your sermon?

We are the dream and the dreamer.
The shout and the stillness.
The hand clap in heaven
that kept the whole thing from falling apart.

And if we vanished?

The country would keep spinning.
But the soul?

It'd stay stuck
on the part of the record
where the needle breaks.

But oh, how you'd miss us
when the protest turned quiet
and your favorite slogans
lost their soundtracks.

You'd miss us
in the absence of flavor,
of footwork,
of forgiveness.

You'd miss us
when your dances fall flat
and your soul food
tastes like shame.

You'd miss us
when your pulpits lack thunder,
your runways lack curve,
and your marches feel off-beat.

We are the griot's echo,
the cradle and the call.
The quilt and the needle.
The sigh in the gospel
and the shoulder in your storm.

You say all lives matter
but tremble when ours show up loud.
You plagiarize the rhythm
but flinch at the rage.
You want the shine
but not the struggle.
The crown
but not the kink.

So we stepped.

---

III

Left you your credit score sermons
and freedom on layaway.
We disappeared like a hush
after a funeral hymn,
like a secret passed in a hush-toned kitchen
you forgot to listen to.

And if we return—
it won't be for your gaze.
We're not a trend.
Not a trope.
Not a resource to mine
for your soul-starved stories.

If we return,
it'll be on our terms.
Drum first.
Fire next.

It'll be in the quiet breath
before a child says their own name
without shrinking.

We'll come back
when the mirror sees us holy,
not heavy.

We'll come back
when the land remembers
who taught it to sing.

But until then—
you'll know.

We were the beat.

## Joy As A Rebellion

Y'all—
the world is on fire.
But we got boots on the ground.
Not with fire hoses—nah, we bringin' fans,
clappin' through like grandma's hands used to do.

What is joy?
The rebellion.

We don't care like we once did.
Used to cry and tuck pain under lids,
mourned like tradition, wore grief like coats—
but joy kept hummin' in the back of our throats.
Bassline steady like Sunday praise,
footwork feelin' like we done got saved.

I'm a Georgia boy, Savannah-bred,
where I learned to two-step through Spanish moss
and trust that joy won't rust.
I come from a place
where aunties spoke in cast iron and tongues,
and soft boys learn to laugh from their lungs—
they thought we stayed quiet or grew cold,
but I kept my giggle—gold and bold.

I move like the beat's built in my bones.
Every go-go bounce got me claimin' my throne.
Mambo sauce drippin' off joy that I eat,
freedom light beam off my bald-headed heat.

I taste joy in half-smokes hot from Ben's,
in sidewalk stages where the rhythm begins.
An Overnight Scenario caught in the breeze,
a nod from a stranger puts me at ease.

Joy be the house track in my chest,
The boom and tac keeps pain in check.
A deep cut sermon from Sedrick or Rodney,

---

Spirit speakin' through a disco dawn.

We marched. We sang. We voted. We prayed.
We danced in the street. We stayed unafraid.
But like Pac said—we tired of askin'.
Joy ain't no handout—it's passion.
It's right. It's rhythm. It's how we survive.
It's our inheritance—sacred and alive.

What is joy?
The rebellion.

This joy is personal. Sacred. Loud.
Me screamin' hallelujah through the thickest crowd.
Protest with rhythm. Resistance with style.
The look we give haters with a confident smile.

It's the uncle at the grill, joke stuck on repeat,
the cousin with two-step glued to his feet.
It's the baby in Spidey shoes shoutin' "see me!"
and me—grown, bald, tender, free.

A man. A brother. A son in his prime.
Built like oak, but I sway with time.
I dap up strangers who feel like kin.
Flexin' through the crowd, Beyoncé hummin' low.

I laugh in the shop where clippers hum truth,
and cry when they buzz over wounds of youth.
I ain't scared to blush. I ain't shy to sing.
I ride shotgun in joy, let the high notes ring.

I love my kin.
We pour out care and drink it back in.
Too much? Maybe. But never enough.
This love's a sermon. This tenderness—tough.

We ain't just surviving—we glowing, we grooving.
Living like liberation already movin'.
Joy is the rhythm, the verse, the beat.

---

The sweat in the set. The heat in the street.

They call us too much—too proud, too loud.
We smile. We strut. We stand unbowed.
Too Black to break. Too bold to shrink.
Too full of praise to care what they think.

>                   What is joy?
>                   The rebellion.

Say it again—

>                   What is joy?
>                   The rebellion.

For the ones who came before.
For the ones who ain't made it home.
For the ones still dancin' in heat of their own.

>                   What is joy?
>                   The rebellion.

So next time they ask how we still here—
tell 'em we danced through the dirt and the fear.
Loved out loud, even when it stung.
Held joy like a secret on the tip of our tongue.

>                   What is joy?
>                   The rebellion.

And I'm still dancin' in it.

## If You're Listening, Nephew; If You're Watching, Niece

Come sit.
World's still spinning,
but you ain't gotta chase it.

Breathe.
Let me tell you what time taught me
when I wasn't looking.

Sexual attention ain't love.
That fire in your skin?
Don't mistake it for a heartbeat.
A mouth on your neck
don't mean a hand on your future.
Some folks'll light you up
just to watch you flicker.

And if they say "maybe"—
baby, that's a no in a tux.
Don't wait for an answer
that already walked away.

Never leave your bed after 1AM
just to be somebody's silence filler.
Nothing holy happens that late
except sleep...or regret.

Love is a verb with work boots on.
It's dishwater hands and "did you eat?"
It's Tuesday arguments that don't end in exits.
It's folding towels
when folding's the last thing you feel like doing.

You want clarity?
Stop translating mixed signals.
Stop decoding maybe's.
The truth don't stutter.

And don't confuse company
with connection.
Some folks hold you
just tight enough
to keep you from leaving—
never tight enough to feel safe.

You worried about not having enough?
Look at your hands.
Your breath. Your ideas.
God don't bless with things—
He blesses with opportunity,
with tools,
with the right nudge at the wrong time
to see if you're paying attention.

You, niece.
You, nephew.
You are the rescue.
You are the resource.
You are not scraps
waiting on someone else's appetite.

And if they show you confusion?
Don't unpack.
Don't water the soil
just 'cause you're standing in it.

Be bold enough to leave folks
where you found them—
not from spite,
but from self-recognition.

And remember.....

Time don't lie.
It don't rush.
But it always reveals.

www.ingramcontent.com/pod-product-compliance
Lightning Source LLC
Chambersburg PA
CBHW022033090426
42741CB00007B/1042